LOVE AND LUST-FILLED LULLABIES

BRADFORD J. GILMORE, MD

LOVE AND LUST-FILLED LULLABIES

iUniverse books may be ordered through booksellers or by contacting:

iUniverse
1663 Liberty Drive
Bloomington, IN 47403
www.iuniverse.com
1-800-Authors (1-800-288-4677)

Because of the dynamic nature of the Internet, any web addresses or links contained in this book may have changed since publication and may no longer be valid. The views expressed in this work are solely those of the author and do not necessarily reflect the views of the publisher, and the publisher hereby disclaims any responsibility for them.

Any people depicted in stock imagery provided by Getty Images are models, and such images are being used for illustrative purposes only.
Certain stock imagery © Getty Images.

ISBN: 978-1-5320-7442-4 (sc)
ISBN: 978-1-5320-7441-7 (e)

Library of Congress Control Number: 2019905188

Print information available on the last page.

iUniverse rev. date: 04/26/2019

CONTENTS

Narcolepsia..1

Anemic in Rivers of Red..3

Alfalfa at Worship...6

Surrounding You My Pearl—Second Version..............................9

Chasing Dandelions Feathers on Blustery Clouds.....................11

Surrounding You My Pearl..14

Green Tis Yon Tidy Farm and Field..16

Etching Back on Walkers' Bay...18

Threshing The Earth..20

Chestnut Of Skin...22

Discovered by Strangers..24

Senior Plague...26

Maiden of Gold..29

Orlando Not Forgotten..31

Snaggled Hair At Church..34

Dripping at Twilight..36

Full Truck..38

Chiseled Fluid..39

God Got Tired of Ogling Stars..41

Fire In Me Bones...43

Eastern Twins...45

United in the Garden...46

Dry Oasis Shore...47

Homesick for the Lamblike Lowly..48

Plunging Waters..50

Shout Wide..51

Summer Winds..53

Travesty of Elder Love...56

The Rainbow of Nature's Seasons...58

The Amorous Seasons..60

A Stroll Through The Seasons... 61

Hurricane Alley.. 63

Caressing Mountains Zenith.. 65

His Lips with Virile Juices... 67

Tender Kisses and Eternal Empires... 69

Fury on Earth... 71

Guarded or Left to Squander.. 73

O Lord, our Lord, surmounting clouds... 75

His Mantle... 77

An Ebony Guy.. 79

Dead Ringer... 81

My Marrow Mate.. 83

Environments' Agendas.. 85

Incandescence.. 86

Snuffing Incandescence.. 88

Aphrodisia and a New Day.. 89

Fruity Friend.. 91

Black Hills of Inky Soil.. 93

Laden With Nectars Shaping Twilight.. 95

Kaleidoscopes Colliding... 98

A Dither of Infectious Blithering in the Public Square.................................. 99

Spring's Dawn.. 101

Our Shepherd! the Lamb of God.. 103

My Smiling Tears Melancholia... 105

Lava Founts Silvery Damp Red.. 106

Entwined... 108

The Triumph: Making Love in Mine Fields... 109

Solitary... 110

Apricot Nectars...111

Alloy Blocking Disunion.. 112

The Voice of the Unutterable Sings... 114

Shrapnel of the Canopy... 117

The Tiles on the Floor.. 119

NARCOLEPSIA

Aphrodite rose, a mere shadow
comparisons only flimsy webs
lamps are dim when you're around
diamond drums dancing streams strum

mirrors burst at Adonis' faces
looking glasses whirl like gyroscopes
gyrations cease crinkled shamrocks bud
as breezy naked feet toe-to-toe waltz by

moonlight halos your face and crown
fierce silver eyes like Persian felines
fuchsia sequents skirt your heaving breast
we the men of the night giddied flames in flight

sparks in feuds between Thanatos and Eros
keys flash for hammock chambers and silk pillows
fettered to trees satin sheets scything swaths
impenetrable egression slithering high tail it

crooning pigeons spy from statue's limbs
Hades hors de combat hobbled Atlas
my cosmos crashing careening into convex caves
you are on the pirate schooner swept beyond twilight

Nodding off and on with part dream and part consciousness... tell me what you think and interpretations
if you wish...a bit demented I know! © a year ago, Brad Gilmore dream • sleep • narcolepsy • mythology

ANEMIC IN RIVERS OF RED

Embers clothed us both at eventide
with smoke imperceivable.
Coals still radiating lava at dawn.

My hair short and burnished brown.
His, the color of strawberries in the wild
with lily white skin be-speckled in cloves.

I whispered exuberantly
"Red, the crimson waves
arrive breaking through to greet us"

Yes, Red and I swam
out in aquamarine waters.
But the stop sign
never squelched our fun.

We played and splashed
alongside the red-velvet coast
dotting it with realgar ash.

In the cliffs of Majolica earth there,
we stalked to see molten streams
of paradise's engorged bosom.

Pausing, we turned toward town.
The jaunt felt timeless
as we abled arm 'n arm
setting out for Maggie Rose's tavern.

Imbibing his usual sangria drenched in burgundy,
Red stood aloft the bar,
speaking coarsely, debating wildly while reciting
Marxist lingo in toto.

Raging, burning with anger and passion,
my friend with flaming irreverence,
buttonholed the first skinhead seen,
though an Aryan giant twice his size.

A quick-tempered flush upon their cheeks
flashed downward engulfing
engorged neck, ruddy torso and belly.
Both with Adonis' ichor and veins bulging
punch each other senseless reaping bright gore
soaking tables, chairs and floor.

The rest gather steam in cannibalistic fashion
yet my Red stands tall while being
pummeled raises the "Sickle and Hammer"!

The Nazis stack up their wounded
bloodied as tomatoes against the brick wall
Red grabs me pulling me through the ****'s door.

Holding his gushing gash,
we make it inside the empty barn,
As I lay him on a bed of hay,
a foreboding pallor descends
masking his rubied flamboyance.

Weakly, he pleads my name.
The butchery now apparent
weeps from wounds like a sieve.

All anger and politics dismissed.
Claret spots envelop his thinly veiled carass.
Salmon ribbons of flesh punctuate the scene.
In anguish, I sob over and over again
Then, I grow ashen while a brumal sweat
frostbites my skin and sinews, muscles and bones.

I shake staring at my bloodless buddy:
eyes fixed, wounds too late for clotting,
necrosing aroma of death...
white turning blue...
anemic in rivers of red.

Fictional characters I made up to write this poem...the characters are quite red in love, emotionally., in politics, intense battling and death caused by wounds hemorrhaging. This pitted against the rouge of a land- and seascapes with hint coming from the celestial sphere. during dawn and dusk. © a year ago, Brad Gilmore friendship-society • death

ALFALFA AT WORSHIP

Fertile fields harvested
sage brush alienated
from tumblin' tumbleweed
weeds grew quietly slyly
in disguise on acres arid

hand picked the farmer so wise
with flaming eyes discerned the ploy
his stratagem clever to the tee
menace weed dances in ripe old age
shedding seed
impregnating native ground

Mimicking authentic the beguiling
plant thought of himself adroit
"the laborers are exhausted
why take sight? Mounting a team,
keeping flowers at bay
the just and the damned did dream

clammy in morning drenched in dew,
fraud one cursed his dream like Cain
but the righteous blessed the Creator

apocalypse drums pulsing through their stems
intensity to bloom will give the weeds away
they throttle truth-speakers

but both bud their blooms
nature could not delay

flowers and leaves burgeoning
with hushed tones, stentorian speech
slander the workers from their bitter roots

blaspheming the owner
skeptically maltreats messenger
Pyrrho housing traitor
subterranean Judas bulb

harvesters ready to pluck
the field until acreage nude
Master examines the tillage

quack grass plotted
to lynch the alfalfa at worship

SURROUNDING YOU MY PEARL—SECOND VERSION

I am an alabaster shell
surrounding you
salinity from founts drizzle
between the clefts

A silvery moon
with sunset halos
ebonies sculpting topaz
in eye goblets

cherry roses bud
bloom tiaras on your breasts
I ladle my lips and tongue
lambently licking gliding swirling

grazing the sea of your dew
arching bridges on pillows
satin juices shimmering warmth
boughs and trunks pool as one

couple waltzing in amber waves
aquamarine foam on burnished slate
draped in iris and indigo powder
you save me from the drowning depths

my petals cling snuggly to you
canoodling increasing pulsation, panting
eyes mist over in sleep
on coral ridges and bussing palms

CHASING DANDELIONS FEATHERS ON BLUSTERY CLOUDS

Chasing dandelions feathers on blustery clouds
so our love used to seem to be
Climbing the mighty oak to its pinnacle in rays of light
so our love is now and forever
longer than the redwoods
stronger than the Rock of Gibraltar
higher than Everest
deeper than the Atlantic
like Atlas bearing the world though together.
swoon at the aquamarine shores in your eyes
melding the infinite and the brittle

hope waltzes atop windowsills
joy in sensuous tango
love the buoyant trampoline
comradery shouldering ages
Achilles shooting arrows at the same target
rowing in sync the same rapids
strolling in the same verdant valley path
naked ones dunked in the same water
bursting fountains of life bosom to bosom

happy the flight of larks
echoes between the stony canopy
kilts a-jig bonnie bagpipes Amazing Grace
shofars blasting out a call of celebration
bands for hands halos for crowns
shattering wedding goblet of new wine under the chuppah
glass slippers after canoodling the arch of your feet
sterile stitches to each other's wounds bandaids trashed

cellars with chains sobbing but not alone
Niagras cresting nose and cheeks blotted out each companion
from dungeons and Loch Ness dragons sprung like jungle frogs to liberty
first, friends on clover looking at the towering cumulous
joining hula-hoops hip to hip
bluegrass dancing in moonlight spooning
on old needlepoint couches and velvet cushions
church bells for the fusion of lads at the altar

Valentine's Day is but one romantic day
the rest of life in amour decorated
opals of kindness peacocks of humility
ambrosia of amethyst synergy
flint and stone with spark
lighting the way for a new Genesis and Exodus

leaving shadowy caverns behind
blackholes explode as we depart
hand in hand

Suicide attempts might have ended my life before my love came into my life. My love saw me through
my emotional derangement. Tenderness and kindness to each other healed our wounds and cemented
our hearts. The struggles we have gone has taken us from diamonds in the rough to well cut gemstones
ready for chuppah discourse. Valentine's Day has its valuable place but is a drop in the bucket while
our devotion is an ocean. © a year ago, Brad Gilmore new-beginnings • love • hope • joy • romance

SURROUNDING YOU MY PEARL

I am albastor shell
surrounding you my pearl
tears of salt drizzle
between the clefts

A silvery moon
with sunset halos
ebonies sculpting topaz
in eye goblets

cherry roses bud
bloom tiaras on your breasts
I ladle my lips and tongue
lambently gliding swirling

grazing the sea of your dew
arching bridges on pillows
satin sluices shimmering warmth
boughs and trunks pool as one

heritage dancing in amber waves
aquamarine foam on burnished slate
draped in iris and indigo powder
you save me from the drowning depths

my petals cling snuggly to you
vacant of strength panting
eyes mist over in sleep
on coral ridges and palms

Thinking of love can take you to richness that Life wants to bring you to and how secure but an utterly dangerous. We often treasure safety far too much and miss the luscious life and love that is worthy of a lot more daring. © a year ago, Brad Gilmore love • nature • adult

GREEN TIS YON TIDY FARM AND FIELD

Green tis yon tidy farm and field
laden with fair fruit maternity's fare..
a bunch of rascals of mix and matchings
renown for hardy, and the hilarious dare!

Laughter raves the quirk-some lot
with generosity's lapping riddling ink
delirious with tongue-in-cheek jests and yarn
a-flit of jokiers' flattery and drunkard's drink

imbibing's yen for snort and chuckle,
does this dazed dozen's mirth with kin inspire
a jolly coughing spree of tee-heed chortles' fancy,
pun-spawned gleeful blithe fun and desire.

These gay, red-nosed and chipper of mankind
with a distinction crisp and clever,
unsinkable in the their festive mood,
spread to those e're about through every kind endeavor

the nature of fraternity bright and rare.
While tucked in the bed of vert acre wild and flowing,
these children in their dreams afresh with jaws
wide gaping, lisp out last laughs while cocks begin a-crowing!

---

sometimes for me to meet a truly good natured and happy soul is so contagious, infectious in laughter
it makes me smile during the day's tough hour...this is an honoring to these wondrous folk
© 2 years ago, Brad Gilmore

ETCHING BACK ON WALKERS' BAY

Stark and still the tyrant clouds roll in
upon the icy steel of walkers' bay
etching back on walkers' bay

The misty sunset cold and fierce
with mounded snow lavender -- pale--
draws in the night with each sighing breath.

As we gaze, my love, at fire flame,
the rosy cast of ember's coal
gleams upon your blushing cheek.

The snowflakes caress your doe eyelashes..
soft, cold, moist, mixed with sea spray
and salted tear linger long at walker's bay.

Clasped in the grasp of tight embrace
we shiver but once, gooseflesh springs erect,
alert to every noise and whisper.

Entwined together the gentle heaving
pulses the cavity to dance and limbs sough
and trunk ruddy, raw aflame awakens sought desire

The tempest is now upon us, my heart,
from without and from within, the tempered rhythm mounts
while the gale howls, crescendoing, exploding climax of Eros.

Panting we arise, resurrected from the "little death"
Poised and birthed a new life together we do take charge
etching back on walker's bay, etching back on walker's bay.

THRESHING THE EARTH

kings and their countries
collapse and fall
vacant steel, brass
and stone

tremble O you nations
tremble O you thrones
for the trampling
of the Almighty

the stumps of them
line the fields of men
shakes and quakes
topple the giant's arms

tremble O you nations
tremble O you thrones
for the trampling
of the Almighty

grapes of wrath
march out justice
for the poor and lowly
as blood fills the valleys

tremble O you nations
tremble O you thrones
for the trampling
of the Almighty

none escapes His view
of this, no one flees
nor hide in caves of rock
nor rest in the shadow of trees

tremble O you nations
tremble O you thrones
for the trampling
of the Almighty

tidal waves sweep
like the besom the nations
crowns float like twigs
At Last!
the terminal threshing
has come

Well, at midterms in studies and had to take a break. I am doing my master's in public health. I just read the Old Testament accounts of Daniel and the troubling dreams and visions of rulers. There truly is One Who will bring down nations and set up empires in wrath because of injustice, social depravity, the weeping of the worker who receives no or little pay. He will bring down industrial giants to protect His earth. Those who destroy the earth and its peoples, He will destroy. He will not turn the blind eye. © 3 months ago, Brad Gilmore society • spiritual • injustice • termination

CHESTNUT OF SKIN

chestnut of skin
raven of hair
porcupine beard
organic man

chocolate bulbs
inky caterpillar bridge
Pantheon nose
David Michelangelo

juicy vermillion smile
ivories pearls aligned
cheeks of peaches
furry cornucopia chin

neck of palm
Ural shoulder mounds
chest billows
connatal man

amorous oak limbs
rapids' stones belly
mahogany buttress
fluidly statuesque

tightly forked boughs
extending root pads
chipmunk feathered toes
erect like redwoods

mysterious sturdy oak partner

The one whom I love is sturdy, loyal and trustworthy. He and I entwined. © a year ago, Brad Gilmore
love • nature

DISCOVERED BY STRANGERS

crunch splatter
slippery leaves
butt fall
diminuendo crash
redwood wall

bouquets of canary oak
sugar maple
crimson poplar
aroma of cedar
emerald Noel's shards
prick my mezmerized
chapped palm

my guiltless
backsliding
careened me to
wonderland
royal crimson maple
aureole beech ladies
Casinova variegated bracts

pungent emanating perfume
wafts in stinging air
cloud burst
thunderstorms
tornadic lightening
stirring leaves
like a witch ladling
potions

my recumbent
anatomy sprawled
against
copper cardinal oak
guarded me
oleaginous autumn
path of alarm
pellets of hail
struck my frame
purple dimples
on my skin erupted
stuporous
discovered by strangers
passing by

How many times do you fall on your rump on slippery leaves? Ever stopped by a tree to be seen by
strangers? © a year ago, Brad Gilmore seasons • nature • autumn-leaves

SENIOR PLAGUE

involutionary melancholia
ground down to pepper specks
pin rolling tremors trembling
faint moans of lament

seductive wheelchair

my era passed into gold
white bobbing heads remain
staring headlight glasses
silent stereo batteries

wrinkled old paper bag

deflated biceps
sagging glutes
vacant delicate curves
sunken tummy
flimsy navel

body mush hangs me tree-ward

dentures clacking
old maids quacking
gents with canes
bent in two
glare at tiles

retirement to the grave

mournful wailing
beating my breast
last day in paradise
youth and summer sky
inkblots tarpit agony

assisted??living??

cankered malaise stalks
miserly measured love-lust
attending amigos
casket writhing
noxious morticians

caustic formic acid transfusion ticking

an hour, a minute
crushing migraine
temples whacked
memory absconders
tissue mutiny

Thor's paddles ineffective---I'm gone

This poem has been written hours before moving to a dinky assisted living apartment. Probably a good idea from a medical standpoint but emotionally feels super creepy and crummy. I have been here before 7 years ago. It was thought surely that I'd be dead by now...I had Parkinson's disease Have been off meds many years and symptoms have not returned (pin-rolling tremors, bobbing head, poor memory, wheelchair bound). But heart, lungs not doing great. Feel I am losing all my youth and purpose which I have to fight otherwise I'll be hanging from some tree. (Picture is me and my first day of chemotherapy for rare leukemia; currently in remission but staying on regimen. © a year ago, Brad Gilmore growing-old • retirement • death • parkinson's-disease • memory-care

MAIDEN OF GOLD

wind-blown golden ropes
spiral on statuesque neck
shoulders burnish mahogany

sea blossoms
grasped ivory
eyelids dance upon

sculpted nuzzler
punctuated colon
reclining pastels

malleable lips
unlatched maw
violet opening orisons

blushed half moons
vales of tears
Wisconsin joyous hills

alabaster teeth ablaze
beckoning tongue
viola mixing soprano

bosoms playing
bouquet belly
hips of a maiden

mons well-forested
untouched cave
entrance exit

mellow thighs
artist's calves
desirous Athenian pillars

Cinderella's glass shoes
ballerina toes
graceful dance Renoir

---

a poets interpretation of all of Pierre-August Renoir © a year ago, Brad Gilmore
beauty • nature • love • painting-renoir

ORLANDO NOT FORGOTTEN

Speaker Big Cheese
at the helm
assorted cheeses

49 slaughtered Orlando
gay, Latinos, and many more
"Pulse"* loaded that night

Those at the helm
gays not referenced
Family, friends horrified

Pulse queer bar
attack by New York joe
second genes here now

Frequent visits to pub
queer fear rampant
second genes across the sea

Armed to the teeth
shots rang
horror
crushed back wall

Dragging palpable mortality
gory entrails sidewalk
blood fountain cascade
slipping glistening puddles
crimson no clots
wailing kith kin
wounded cops
dripping scarlet rags

azure cheery-red flashing
ivory box vehicles
pale corpse wide-eyed

one cheese right
one cheese left
platforms NOT people
guns religions blamed

Machiavelli manupulation
fear of Islam thick jam
wrath to guns dense fog

Speaker!
Put the anchor down!
weep and wail
sons daughters interred

time for eye to eye
epoch bridges
surfaced walls

tornado election
baby candidates
soiled diapers
have to be changed first

Orlando cries forgotten
passerby passing by
your lives still matter to me
my friends

---

*Pulse is the predominantly gay night club in Orlando
We forget too easily those killed by people estranged from each other...there is no murder justified,
no slaughter is G-d's will. May by grace sit down and know each other well before hate talk starts. ©
a year ago, Brad Gilmore pain • sad • society • family
Like (2)

SNAGGLED HAIR AT CHURCH

snaggled hair
clad in bib overalls
outside the church stairs
hiding smokes
in tee-shirt sleeves
I peered in

no other shaggy dudes
some with Amish bonnets
nursing cherubs in back rows
others sporting suspenders
boys and girls ruddy cheeks and toes
friends, sisters, brothers

my eyes effusive and red
a bit from Mary Jane
more from open arms and bright smiles
young hippie folk cross-legged
sitting on the brick slabs
guitarist hallowed the scene

four-part harmony of tongues inflight
muted lightbulbs with Bibles turning pages
explosive gospel man's honey
air waxed clean babies chiming
hours skipped by in a sunlit night
at seventeen, my first church stroll

My first experience at church did not occur until late adolescence for me...unlike some, the warmth of God's Presence was overwhelming and church meeting didn't end until about literally six hours from start to finish and was going on strong for the four years almost everyday when I was there and a youth. Changed my life and drug addiction disappeared in a flash for me. Started drinking when I was 9 with a schoolfriend moving into deeper drugs and ended at 17 with my first visit to church.

The picture is of me © 6 months ago, Brad Gilmore love • spiritual • jesus-christ • church • jesus-people

DRIPPING AT TWILIGHT

myself, a pivotal droplet
my mama was rain
my papa the sea mist
in the Water family

I joined, splashed
with scores of my twins
streamed to cusp
of the canary bud

I sink into the earth
journeying deep
forging gorges
sculpting canyons

Adam's ale yielding
to the oak, the sow,
the elephant, the whale
quaff dew, drink from troughs
cooling.earth's crust
mammoths' showering eructation

the essential element of life
is not technology
nor medical breakthroughs, no,
it's me dripping at twilight.

We all need a purpose for living to be essential to life. We can join others in significance as well as be
irritatingly alone working at night, Who you are, is indistinguishable from action and purpose you bring
to the earth. © 7 months ago, Brad Gilmore nature • intrinsic--worth • independence • union • water

FULL TRUCK

collard greens
hominy and grits
black-eyed peas
peaches cherry pits

Miss Carolina's
market day
rickety Ford
fieldhands' hay

sweet kernel corn
chunky plucked hen
spuds by the barrel
full truck home again

© 10 months ago, Brad Gilmore hope • family • rhyme

CHISELED FLUID

The future belongs to those who believe in the beauty of their dreams.

trembling
eyes flooding
lips skirting forehead

streams trickling
temples drumming
grins of milk
hammocked
cheek bridging cheek

from faraway shores
cuddled scratchy chin
spiciest salsa
uncoiled stretches
starched wrinkled clothes
eyelashes
feather my neck

no make-up
cosmetics disappear
masks flung
in flames licking
storming
chiseled fluid now

GOD GOT TIRED OF OGLING STARS

God got tired of ogling
all the stars in space
glued together one
that really took the cake
His syncretistic imagination
the star for Bethlehem did make

flickering flare in the midnight sky
treble cleft for cherubim and seraphim
cradling the holy neonate
lambs roared at the beam
seers and soothsayers
to see the King come to redeem

so the story goes
to drunken bridal shower
agua into regal champagne
demonstrates His gawking power
so requests poured in from every port
lushed new wine the gluttons devour

JC did not stop there
along the merry road
blind eyes divined open
at Zaccheus's house abode
after JC came the avaricious puny man
uncorked wallet with coins a-flowing

cresting water's tide came strolling
scared his men beyond their wits
"Holy smokes! Poseidon has appeared!"
"Fear not! T"is I" the terror by Jesus Christ remits
the tempest brewing just fell asleep instead
on the cross in death, in hell, all. our sin JC acquits

ruthless tyrants come and go
and in spirit, they are slaughtered
but bedraggled weary ones like us
and orphan-types alone are fathered
JC is coming soon that's something I do declare
to a simple peace to which we're called
while other brothers just won't be bothered

---

this contest poem sprung from the work of Magiclight and is entitled ""The JC Show".This is a little sequel to it © a year ago, Brad Gilmore love

FIRE IN ME BONES

fire in me bones
no one knows
glazing ice pendulums
belt down grows

tame me undomesticated me
burgeoning lavender
pursue in scarlet flame
a tasty scavenger

chase me around the buttress
and bridge me to you
askance if you must
my head is thick with dew

you are a must blanket
resting on my inflamed breast
heaving sighs and moans
rough sandpaper across me chest

ocean spray against open cheeks
all grins at your homecoming pigeon
smoldering flint dashes on the rocks
torsos glistening honey full smidgen

kiss me high kiss me low
my wringling neck poised for sultry tongue
salty vigor springs the bunny out his hole
trembling limbs gliding mysteries hung...unsung

Note: "me" bones and "me" chest are intentional © a year ago, Brad Gilmore
love • relationship • making-love

EASTERN TWINS

You are the most numerous
upon this spinning blue marble.
your aeons of dynasties now
under a scarlet people's banner
aureate spread on your skin

Side by side with the subcontinent
spitting Mt. Everest pinnacles
the smooth chocolate dermal
bark on you
turbins cover your crows' brows
monsoon land of Ghandi and Taj Mahal

the territories of the East
each rams knocking heads
giant Asian fraternal twins

Asia: The 2 most populate nations in the word © a year ago, Brad Gilmore asia

UNITED IN THE GARDEN

Journey on the path of heather
smell the lilac and honeysuckle
eye the cardinal and hummingbird
willows brush their hair by sun and breeze

snuggle up to the breast of Nature
milk in buxom charmers in the periwinkle canopy
puddles full of dawn's dew

stretching out along the esplanade
the beckoning of the waves caress in delicious salt
my siesta is complete and calm

mackerel skiing dolphins' grins
with ity-bitty razors and skin as tough as granite
sea gulls inspect the shoreline's prey

Creator has made us all an Eden
united in holy matrimony unbreakable
He said "It is good, very good!"

Hope you feel the way I feel...contented. Enjoy! © a year ago, Brad Gilmore

DRY OASIS SHORE

Gazelles ballet on mountains rough
lead on the dancing highways for rams tough
Rainbow peacocks strutt their lofty colors
Nightingales in treble key sopranos
Lions countering bass stentorium echoes

Mountain cats and goats quiet and lone
Rattlesnakes' and desert scorpions' tones
Make the earth quake mountains melt
Panoramas of Mother Nature profoundly felt

Ricochets of blasting volcano molten spurts
in stellar display of exploding earthy alerts
the meek wild waters trip and wander
among the granite stones grow fonder

God's breath spans out far and wide
from coasts to coasts the even'tide
His glories, gust and vicarious gore
Sing out loud, sigh, from dry oasis shore.

Thinking about the wildness of creation far outside our control. We can only observe and listen
Awesome isn't it? © a year ago, Brad Gilmore

HOMESICK FOR THE LAMBLIKE LOWLY

society shuns
the simple girl's nerve
narcissistic nuns
deride the meeks' verve

Anabaptists attracting
donate to the dry branch
wisdom wims winnows
on amor's avalanche

ascetic appetite
with sawdust wheat
sans satin sheets
sans Wall Street

Big Ben
ticks night fruits
juggling jogging
progress back to roots

fickle follies
left with napkins' guts
tossed tabletop too
hustling to humble huts
we're homesick for the lamblike lowly

<hr />

This quoted from 1 Corinthians 13:
(ἀγάπη, agape, love and charity)
Though I speak with the tongues of men and of angels, and have not charity (ἀγάπη, agape), I am become as sounding brass, or a tinkling cymbal.
And though I have the gift of prophecy, and understand all mysteries, and all knowledge; and though I have all faith, so that I could remove mountains, and have not charity (ἀγάπη, agape), I am nothing.
And though I bestow all my goods to feed the poor, and though I give my body to be burned, and have not charity (ἀγάπη, agape), it profiteth me nothing.
Charity (ἀγάπη, agape) suffereth long, and is kind; charity envieth not; charity(ἀγάπη, agape) vaunts not itself, is not puffed up,
Does not behave itself unseemly, seeketh not her own, is not easily provoked, thinketh no evil;
Rejoices not in iniquity, but rejoiceth in the truth;
Bears all things, believes all things, hopes all things, endures all things.
Charity (ἀγάπη, agape) never fails: but whether there be prophecies, they shall fail; whether there be tongues, they shall cease; whether there be knowledge, it shall vanish away.
For we know in part, and we prophesy in part.
But when that which is perfect is come, then that which is in part shall be done away.
When I was a child, I spoke as a child, I understood as a child, I thought as a child: but when I became a man, I put away childish things.
ἀγάπη agápē;
I am drawn to the simple life out the contemptuous complexities leading to ultimate catastrophe and the mortal and moral demise of the human spirit. No one can think for herself or himself especially outside the box. Can there be diversity and not conformity? Seeking the simple life is to leave for uncharted waters and love liberty of thought, loving others as you love yourself living the humility to listen to others' needs and problems and ideas. A life moved receiving juniority following despite the obstacles.To be tough yet tender, tenacious tendency, tamed remembrances and meekly resilient. Most of us tend to be hogs with rings in our. Seek a simple, thought-filled life. © 11 months ago, Brad Gilmore rhyme • society • simplicity • love • free-thinking

PLUNGING WATERS

Raindrops
Rain in puddles
Baptized
Chance
Fingers of rescue
Tug softly
From gulping waters?

SHOUT WIDE

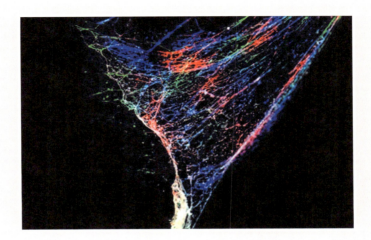

Shadows and mirrors
Gilded leaf bed posts
cob-webbed canopy
sultry eve's peaches
aromas mean fanfare

Don your periwinkle sash
I'll tame my black mustache
You feather your eyelash
Shout wide our brash pash.

Top hats and lacy bonnets
bowties and emerald charms
crimson vest, cufflinks white cuffs
pantaloons and garter belts
raven curls and blonde wigs

Don your periwinkle sash
I'll tame my black mustache
You feather your eyelash
Shout wide our brash pash.

Mawkish tunes on ole Victrola
Blue Danube waltzes four-step
My pipe and Bourboned ice
seduce me with hints of Burberry
sachet and pearly jump ropes

Don your periwinkle sash
I'll tame my black mustache
You feather your eyelash
Shout wide our brash pash.

Senile minds can only remember
Youth ones only permit nightdreams
Yet in yesteryear all dress up....
all play and "make believes" come true
Your carriage awaits mademoisselle

Don your periwinkle sash
I'll tame my black mustache
You feather your eyelash
Shout wide our brash pash.

Total silly recall of "make believes" and "dress-ups" placed on us seniors © a year ago, Brad Gilmore
<u>humor</u> • <u>'make-beliefs'</u> • <u>age</u>
Like (2)

SUMMER WINDS

attributes
we find cute
will soon
balloon
and bust
to dust

fireworks
for some perks
blast in full array
on display
sparks
bring thunderous remarks

the band's blast
commencing fast
college diploma
embroidered for pa and ma
grandkids prance
grandpas dance

victory
showered confetti
tie-dyed shirts
ankle high miniskirts
stilettos
fond mementos

ice cream sops
whirling lollipops
cotton candy
the prom's dandy
up pops pride
splashing waterslide

wave pool rush
dripping swim trunks tush
orchard smells
kissing spells
picnic aprons
misty dawns

lightening flashes
homeward dashes
sunburn blisters
homefolk sisters
beaching bombshells
cold shower quells

vegetable bed
azaleas spread
lilac lark
ivory birches bark
o yes my dear
summer's here

Though we may "vacation" in the summer there is a swirl of activity and locomotion every which way! Get this from just my little schedule: Memorial Day, my grandson's 3rd birthday (all he can think about is "potty"!...hahaha); middle son graduated from college and has one week before his Master's program begins...commencement today; Father's Day; this week my oldest turns 40!; next week get to see my youngest grandson whom I haven't yet held...born on Christmas Eve...; good friend gets married on June 30; see parade; 4th of July; interviews; enrollment....sister knocking on 70th year...Labor Day...Fast paced to Autumn on the dread of MN winter....I am enjoying summer despite the heat and humidity here! Stay cool! © 9 months ago, Brad Gilmore
rhyme • summer • seasonal • celebrations • fun

TRAVESTY OF ELDER LOVE

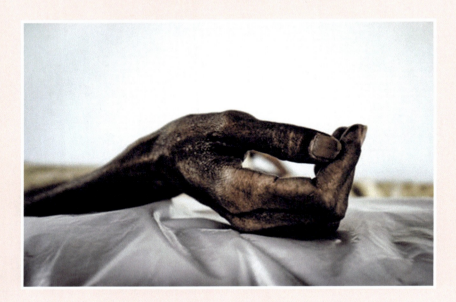

Grey hair and balding with bun clung to her fragile scalp
this matriarch perched upon the thread bare chair
knitting, brooding, waiting for embraces in her last days

Spending time nights genuflecting
upon her feeble knees with rosary in hand
squeezing crucifix and beads in moans
of Our Fathers and Hail Marys

"My G-d and I will soon gape at one another face to face!"
but downward her gaze unable raise her brows..humped were her shoulders
her back in ceaseless agony covered her grandest blouse
now dolefully embroidered and sheer stripped in outmoded glory

Forsaken in the nursing home with bed pans as companions..
like these, her comrades she hoards the excrement of life in her vessel.
Abandoned by her kids and little known by their teeny tots

Gramps in his beleaguered slouch attached by posey to the wheelchair
still picking off egg and toast crumbs from yesterday's breakfast
with his hands full of tremors and knuckles gnarled in rheumatism.

He has oft times tried release himself from these oppressive straps
or pull out the Foley until blood spouted from his loins.
Bleak hospice is in his cards and unrest in his bones.

At once his grey eyes and hers aquamarine hugged at a distance
Sparkles of tenderness and empathy were exchanged
Saline dropped from their eyes reading out loud boldly "Paradise"

Gramps spun the wheels of his power chair ambling beside la dame.
Startled by his warmth and speed, a blush filtered through her pale face.
Extending his palm, he clasped her meaty freezing mitts.

Fragrances of denture breath mixed with the lingering Dentine
they did not despise their crusty lips...they marveled.. they kissed
again and again buoyantly tingling from head to toe
gleaming spirits grinning side to side

Alas, my dear, alas how fervent their ardor as dusk approached!
Gently as he lay against her fair bosom
They breathed their last, they breathed their last and passed.

I used to be an orderly on a geriatric floor...and occasionally be able to view a scene or 2 like this....
now in my 60s I relate to it more and more © 2 years ago, Brad Gilmore

THE RAINBOW OF NATURE'S SEASONS

ebony crows upon the pallid branch
claspsing necrotic* arboreal flesh
for winter's breath fixed freeze
adhering the bird flush with the twig

like the day cyclicly rounds spinning in time
the day begins after midnight with inky sky
winter commences
the end of the calendar
beginning of the new year

creating the worlds out of darkness
and void in the vacuum of the clock moving rapidly
to an apocalyptic end,, we all return
to darkness with emptiness..bitter

chasing away daftly the shadow of the nighttime
killing the Siberian frost murdering every lingering nightmare
evidence hope sprouting from verdant grasses
and tulips of crimson flame, lemon, violet petals

ah, yes this is new birth and resurrection
springtime reminds us that life begins beneath the soil
nocturnal birds chant the undying remarks and probes
of self awareness "who"

on the limbs alabaster buds blossom intensifying
oncoming emerald leaves and snow flowers
peach, apple and cranberry trees showing off
in full bloom like high school sweethearts in the park

gleaming summer beams lance through the hot summer air
thrilling the young at heart to explore waters
unavailable the rest of the year demanding tans to be made
amidst summertime and swimmings turning skins to fur of foxes

following national holidays with strawberry ice cream cones
autumn raps at the door with its demands for harvest moons and rains
with its harvest of grains, veggies, fruit and holy celebrations
chestnut chipmunks chase after acorn

cresting with a bouquet of leaves:
scarlet, amber, chestnut and bile colored
evergreen needles cloistered in hand.

hay rides, amber straw filled farms,
golden pollen filled ambiance and mossy molding bark
along with campfires to cuddle by and tell ghost stories

---

the aroma of fall brings on the lament of Yuletide to repeat again
Entered into Nature's Four Seasons © 2 years ago, Brad Gilmore

THE AMOROUS SEASONS

grey misty eyes glisten
to pounding hearts listen
ruddy sweating on satin
moisten in Spring's verdant fields

fuschia tongues entwined
punctate nipples aligned
juicy layers hugged flatten
lushed in Summer's breath yields

virgin cherries soupy mix
whipped topping affixed
enraptured firstlings straddle
on Autumn's gold-leaf amour wields

plumed peacock strutting fire
grand pheasant's buds desire
'round holly pricks and mistletoe
December iced ivory sybaritic appeals

A STROLL THROUGH THE SEASONS

lattice of icicles
drops of Spring
violet crocus tulips
honeysuckle butterflies

journey to canary leaves
and crackling twigs
champions of crimson
breath of cold rain

sunflower rubber skins
wipers hypnosis
thunders tornados
dripping shelters

wolves chants
frowning pumpkins
raindrop-snowflake twist
cyanotic shaking

shadows sprawl out
rotating of owl's head
billowy ivory-cast roofs
steamed windowpanes

More than not my thoughts and anxieties come to rest walking from season to season. I believe that is why Jesus when talking about a cure for worry and fear saying "Consider the birds of the .... and flowers of the field...I hope you find peacefulness in this poem © 7 months ago, Brad Gilmore

HURRICANE ALLEY

tumults gather
storm clouds thunder
wailing seas
gulp in frighted wonder

earth's melting
polar caps receding
oceans bubble
bombers not retreating

climate calamity
humans meet their end
hurricane season
electric nails descend

lighthouses beaming
drowned men bob in the tide
women kids screaming
fuzes lit explode on our side

Again, the hurricane sisters and season are upon us while the Gulf boils with hotter, hotter water which lead to greater and greater storms. Mother Nature's daughters won't sleep well until the environment is cleansed of the warring destruction of earth. May God have mercy in the land causing the climate to change and the other ones who have their hands tied to rescue earth. © 8 months ago, Brad Gilmore

CARESSING MOUNTAINS ZENITH

eye catches eye
your head rotates on its spindle
our chests flush robin red
erecting impotent inclinations

motions tell me "Come"
I dog lap you like a fevered pup
your hand strokes my scalp
pin rolling each lock, each curl

kissing head
sucking neck
licking me like a lollipop
I moan

I open mouth
beckon with gliding tongue
our lips introduce themselves
I hold the door open

our panting bodies
fill queen bed
scarlet satin sheets with light splatters
keyed the gate
into secret chamber

our moans as a symphony
consecutive sounds interlock
blazing sweat puddles
virile juices geyser explode

stuck together
entrance open
filling your well with ivory creamy syrup
and caress mountain zeniths

contract contact commencement loots covenant

Prompt 1 was improvised on. Togetherness rather than individual exploitation. I am unable to read my poem. Please read it for me. Thanks © a year ago, Brad Gilmore

HIS LIPS WITH VIRILE JUICES

Dripping with deep overtones
he breathes long and damp,
sonorous and stentorian,
licking softly his lips with virile juices..

South Carolinian tones with titches
of Castilian flavored canticles,
my baritone cantor doused
on the sandlewood streets of Marseilles.

His trumpeting voice of Reveille
awakens my shivers with sprite.
Hair erect on ruby gooseflesh.
His oration launches Titanics.

On the other side of distant waters,
his eyes gaze my length and breadth
from afar with tickling whispers.

Naked neck with pearls of sweat
humming, vibrating with each phrase.
My face waxes cardinal
while I stutter with a desert mouth.

Melodies swim tinward on my tide.
I squirm. I plunge impetuously.
Intoxicated with music from his throat,
my eyes close. I swoon.

Remembrances of each embrace--
each of his stretches burst into view.
His romantic, aromatic speech
quickens my malluability.

He converses with me intimately
like sleeping outside on verdant hills
gazing at stars and moon until sunrise.
Articulating, his opal facets fasten on me.

I am undone yet macho and ready.
"Come home, my Atlas,
and carry me, only me."

TENDER KISSES AND
ETERNAL EMPIRES

tender kisses
snowflakes caressing
eyelashes
cherry cheeks brighten.

dazzling albino drifts
mirroring luminescence
solar
eclipses with the moon

raspberry sunsets
citrus dawns
blazing
midday sun

fragrant mists
of ocean's breath
breakers
alabaster foam

crunching leaves
bouquet amber
glory
wool threads

delicate blooms
erotic dew
rainbows
refreshing rains

surrounding seasons
clicking clocks
calendars
eternal empires

FURY ON EARTH

merciless clouds roll in
hail breaks windows
lightening
shadowing aftermath

horrors of the winds
Boreus blasts snow
championing
blizzard's depths

whirling twirling
cyclones abyss
unsteady
fall into aqua salt

swell on ocean view
Goliath tidal waves
tsunamis
hurricane floods

cracking rock
earthquakes tremble
volcanos
climax annatto spraying

flooded valleys
dustbowl plains
sun
scorching sands

Terrors on earth fascinate me with their impetuous vigor and power and majesty © a year ago, Brad
Gilmore

GUARDED OR LEFT TO SQUANDER

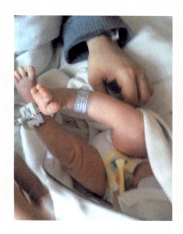

wrapped in pages of pink and baby blue
infant paws are growing
newborns' thumbs wrap around and through
the ventilators blowing

teeny tubes of blood by vampires stolen
lie in heaps a incubator's end
from scalp, neonatal navel and Achilles heel so swollen
to diagnose and to mend.

are we not ready more than are cops
to serve and to protect the number one?

from birthing table to the box of incubation
wee little ones grow fat and long.
bili-lights ward off jaundice, the Persian melon,
that cause that a mosh of brain go wrong

from premie birth through epochs old
it warrants one to say and ponder
how history and destiny wound together will unfold
how will the treasures held here today be guarded or left to squander

O LORD, OUR LORD, SURMOUNTING CLOUDS

O Lord, our Lord, surmounting clouds
Your Name's eclipses the galaxies.
Out of infants suckling the breast
you built secure dwellings
from our foe and the lynching rider

As I ponder the universe's whirling planets,
which You fingerpaint into being
the moon, the stars punctuated
by Your signet ring blot

Why is humanity worth Your while?
Why do You come and visit us?
Men and women You formed
lead creation rising above it

All livestock and fields, waves and mist
eagles and skylark, whales and minnows
octopi and eel, jellyfish and coral
are championed by them and their heroes.

Lord, our Lord, mastering the earth.

My modern day rendition of Psalm 8

Here is Psalm 8 in KJV (1611)
O Lord our Lord, how excellent is thy name in all the earth! who hast set thy glory above the heavens.
Out of the mouth of babes and sucklings hast thou ordained strength because of thine enemies, that thou mightest still the enemy and the avenger.
When I consider thy heavens, the work of thy fingers, the moon and the stars, which thou hast ordained;
What is man, that thou art mindful of him? and the son of man, that thou visitest him?
For thou hast made him a little lower than the angels, and hast crowned him with glory and honor.
Thou madest him to have dominion over the works of thy hands; thou hast put all things under his feet:
All sheep and oxen, yea, and the beasts of the field;
The fowl of the air, and the fish of the sea, and whatsoever passeth through the paths of the seas.
O Lord our Lord, how excellent is thy name in all the earth!

HIS MANTLE

Your Shadow is my light
Your Setting is my rising
my arms too short
to waltz upon the waters

sparklers flicker in my infant vision
the diapers of my shallowness
crescendos electrified gleaming
cupped in the hands of largess

slow dancing with My Chief
brushing my cheek on his chest
His Cor my corridor to God
the clotted imprint of me in His gash

shivering solace
hallowed hiding place
drawing near He pulls
me out of my quivering pulses

crystal founts lick my eyelashes
my pain withers when He's here
Yeshua's mantle full of dew
my eyes dried

welcome home, son

AN EBONY GUY

my papa's,
you see, an ebony guy
we match

his smile awakens the day
my dad's shadow tall
he's a goliath

Gabriel rested me 'round
the noir column
poised on black steel

'neath his night bridges
charcoal eyes
burn brilliant tapestry

a broad inky umbrella
where eyeglasses lie
harness cheek to cheek

father chuckles loudly
his mouth roars like lions
sings snores sonorously

rap tip-toes his muse
boogies around like fire
smoke chases his tail

his breast an iron shield
nothing can rattle it
whirling sables nest I tickle

lap hammock between sequoia
a Golden Gate sans gold
head there exploring dreams

frolicking horse play
I won't let him go
no, not for anything

An Afro-American playful dad is such a royal treasure to behold. I loved this picture so wrote about it. © a year ago, Brad Gilmore

DEAD RINGER

they called me a "dead-ringer"
sent down in coffin nailed securely
with nothing but a silver bell
rocks, sod above done prematurely?

yanking on the earthy chain
their earplugs attending dirge's
droning suffocating cloud
scurrilous formaldehyde scourge

the poison did not slam life's door
but frigid deranged limbs immobile
hard as I pulled the mute alarm
ushered no one to my Chernobyl

bradycardia tones hollow chest bound
brain decomposing, cyanotic, Stoic
buried statue, iconic, fixed eyes azure
like an indigo champion man, heroic

an infant crawling collided with box
tiny fists a' pounding and unshakable bawling
nails shot off the casket fireworks locks
then dragged me to safety crawling

on knees and hands reborn and new
slobbering spittle mouthing praise
inaudibly in a gibberish tongue
and so I am alive, yes, I did raise.

Someday the nails will. pop off and the dead will be raised formaldehyde and all. For all a bodily
resurrection...not just a spiritual ascension is what I believe...the Child by intercession will awaken
all! © a year ago, Brad Gilmore spiritual-love • death

MY MARROW MATE

mahogany melancholic eyes
in chiseled chestnut sockets
to engild blessing buttons on face
tenderest tempered glance

smiles of angelic empathy
lips of utter cuddled compassion
lingua dripping crystalline kindness
voice heralding our wondrous God

Dearest brother
Champion friend
Intimate love
My marrow mate

iron shielding shoulders
black bear burly breast
breathing out sonorous song
clipping clicking cardiac clock

drizzling cavernous axillae
furrowed belly brazen clusters
of dewy Ozarks' melodic muscles
narrowing delta wrapping belt

Dearest brother
Champion friend
Intimate love
My marrow mate

My most trusted and supportive comrade. My chaste cloistered confidential camaraderie © a year
ago, Brad Gilmore

ENVIRONMENTS' AGENDAS

agenda's peril
melting Himalayas
rising sea levels
stranded bears
a floating artic

fossil fuel feud
petroleum exploitation
environmental forsaking
Paris convention detention
laughing stock of the world

huggin trees
picking vines.
fresh and finest
local

healthy bodies
medicine in herbs
halting Big Pharma
FDA letting crap in
FDA keeping gems out

© a year ago, Brad Gilmore

INCANDESCENCE

Shadows
hiding under rocks
sealing caverns
lying in muck
Shadows

Shadows
stumbling stones
slaying civilians
rotten fruits
bread mossy
Shadows

Shadows
whispers loud
slanderous secrets
treacherous billows
drowning pallor
Shadows

Light
brilliance
breaking bread
clothing the naked
employing the homeless
befriending the fatherless
Light

Light
discovering snares
disembarrass deadweight
strolling on Everests
celestial glee
prostrate
Light

Light
incandescence
Master hovers
cherubim ballet
ransom satisfied
invisible sprinkling
Light

Came to mind after reading a passage In Isaiah 9:1-7. We shield ourselves from criticism, underestimate our beliefs, conceal wrongdoings. Coming to the Light face forward we can leave shadows, dark paths and grimy ways. Don't have hide your shadows beneath shadows. © a year ago, Brad Gilmore

SNUFFING INCANDESCENCE

Youngest candle
Flame once sun-like
Needles in deep wax
Scarlet drops continue
Dripping when incandescence

Snuffed ribbon vapor
It's over now
another cracked
candle for the dumpster

now let us try that again

APHRODISIA AND A NEW DAY

aphrodisia
rose and lilly balm
waffs pearly chestnut trunk
caressing succulent tree
midnight strands of hair tease
dripping ambrosia

emerald mirrors
peering globes
whisper intimate chants
through labial sunsets
and tooth pastey smiles

twin mammary volcanos
tempt, excite touch
curving road
dives southward
child emerges
birthing a new day

FRUITY FRIEND

curvature
tooth pasty smile
sweet apple breath
supple cherry lips
parted

strawberry tongue
cheeks peaches
dimpled spud chin
arched inky caterpillar
chestnut eyes

ebony facial field
blackberry cliff
falls on rambutan breast
tight nipple fruit*
date vortexed

you're just plain yummy

Poetic abstract art of close friend
* nipple fruit is an actual fruit, but strange appearance...google it or Wikipedia it... © a year ago,
Brad Gilmore

BLACK HILLS OF INKY SOIL

Black Hills of inky soil
coal and bane ruffle heavens
magnificent ebony breasts
lurching thundering

crackle erupted
night broke open
campfire clouds
stuck to our shadows

dark slippery slate
compound the threat
oblique caverns
abyss open mouths

a young girl
hurled headlong
charred from head to feet
our nares flared

the darkest of crimes
denigrated child of Africa
bitterly frozen abdumbuation
necrotic skin peeled away

Our pupils dilated
picked up
every charcoal detail
remote campfire's smoke

Living in MN the Black Hills are not so far away in South Dakota. Initially a treaty with Native Americans was agreed upon.
Soon, thereafter, there was gold rush displacing the Natives from there land again. Now there are other places in the Dakotas that natural resources and tribes are being exploited. The story is a symbol of events then and now. © a year ago, Brad Gilmore

LADEN WITH NECTARS
SHAPING TWILIGHT

laden with nectars
plums, peaches, pears
shimmering figs
of rainbow shallows

tramps of breezes
hitching on winds
drip ambrosia

you stretched out
me shirtless
the lure of your delicious lips

on my skin delays

abutting oak trunk
you plucking small lilac
pedals on my tongue

eclipse spotlight wicks
moon in audience
moving mounts of satin
shaping twilight

_____

for my love © a year ago, Brad Gilmore

97

KALEIDOSCOPES COLLIDING

Kaleidoscopes colliding
does your lavender-indigo outshine
my noncomplex green

The color of the rainforest and evergreen
protects the colored virtue of diverse flower beds
My color foams aquamarine among emeralds of the sea

Transparent dew colored eyes ever lustful
as I gaze your peacock skin
I love the naked chameleon on my moss covered walls

Though you are purple and I distant green
we share our cyanotic mother
my dad golden hot and your father a furious redneck

So give me the springtime grasses and loamy vales
I will harvest the lilac for you and fill your carriage with amethyst
we both will bloom at mid year and sleep in November

My color is green and yours is purple © a year ago, Brad Gilmore nature • friendship

A DITHER OF INFECTIOUS
BLITHERING IN THE PUBLIC SQUARE

syphilitic swelters in sleeping sacks
smallpox swerves off beaten tracks
delicate dimensions of bio-death

tuberculosis transits traverse the globe
tumors travail transvestites ail in strobe
febrile festering fuming fighting fiercely

Chaucer champions cholera choked
and chance be the chimpanzee croaked
hailed SIV to hover HIV humans to discover

plagues progress to pyres of the poor
pantheon's progroms of pilgrims prevail
multiple mutilations murdering populations

Plagues are not a thing of the past. They are knocking at our front, back and side doors, down the chimneys and up the stairs... Unless we act responsibly, quickly, antiseptically and with due financial diligence, the diseases we face now will pale in comparison the devastation we may see. Mega- bugs with antibiotic resistant strains threaten to return us to days of Pasteur and Jenner. © 7 months ago, Brad Gilmore rhyme • infections • plague • epidemic • death

SPRING'S DAWN

ray pillars bright and gold
lacerating morning's fog
bold breezes abduct
chiffon drapes in cancan
on kitchen's windowsill

over the porcelain sink
aroma of Spring's party
wafts waving lily drink
squinting eyes waltz
with the Master Himself

unbroken swinging voice
hummingbird and cardinal
resurrecting sleepyheads
graves' bedsheats mountains
their future blanket mantle
again when twilight stares through

happier than a lark at harvest
heaven's cornucoplia billows
eyes gleam streams crystal
cresting my nose my cheeks
my mouth full of symphonies
Handel's halleluia chorus

glad to be back in God's hands
business work laundry have to wait
immanent Presence cloaks me
unlacing my shoes socks tossed
viewing His Holiness the first time
broken a man undone by Beauty
waterfalls strolling pause watch
my hands on face absorb Light

I often cry with holy, separate moments.

I write mostly about other human beings and their activities. Today I was overwhelmed by beauty indescribable and burst out of the ground like a new crocus. Like the Lazarus from the Bible, I was resurrected from the dark, murky mundane and placed by the Light, Beauty Himself. Glorious day! Writing this from that ongoing experience and perspective that I found your contest. Thanks! © a year ago, Brad Gilmore

OUR SHEPHERD! THE LAMB OF GOD

Our Shepherd, Lamb of God!
King of the Jews sealed in blood!
Execution for our flesh execrably,
On Golgatha's tree hanged abhorrently.

Chorus: Cursed was He* for me,
He scapegoated to cure our incredulity

This was in no mawkish passion play!
God's love exploded on display!
Stony tablets aided us naught.
only rehearsing our jeopardy caught.

Crushed in the winepress of God's dread
On the mill stone for flax and bread

Flour for His battered, abused Core
Wine for new covenant in His Gore
Oil for His Spirit-anointing
Priestly king by appointing

Murdered for our slaughters
Convicting Presence not perjurers
Compassion annulling our apathy

Mortality ascension immutability.

---

20 lines...Thanks for always reminding of us of our condition and His sacrifice. May the Presence of Messiah be with you If you'd like, the best hymn for this verse is: "O Sacred Headed Now Wounded" in my opinion. Here are some of the words:

O sacred Head, now wounded,
With grief and shame weighed down,
Now scornfully surrounded
With thorns, thine only crown:
How pale thou art with anguish,
With sore abuse and scorn!
How does that visage languish
Which once was bright as morn!

What thou, my Lord, has suffered
Was all for sinners' gain;
Mine, mine was the transgression,
But thine the deadly pain.
Lo, here I fall, my Savior!
'Tis I deserve thy place;
Look on me with thy favor,
Vouchsafe to me thy grace.

What language shall I borrow
To thank thee, dearest friend,
For this thy dying sorrow,
Thy pity without end?
O make me thine forever;
And should I fainting be, Lord, let me never, never Outlive my love for thee. © a year ago, Brad Gilmore

MY SMILING TEARS MELANCHOLIA

golden breeze wafts aromas from afar
are you to come home on sandlewood
with ivory oars and plum feathers?

are you lost and lone on distant banks
or caught in crags and in cold caverns,
adrift, forelorn, no blanket for cover?

will your song ascend the earthly dove?
scattered pigeons pluck and scurry still
in market square like you were there

the mist of October winds cling to branch and twig
I warm myself 'round embers' light, hearth's home,
and entertain the little ones with my smiling tears.

one by one

———————————
Missing a fair love and thinking about children

LAVA FOUNTS SILVERY DAMP RED

hot blazes enflame my rouge drunk head
earthquakes rigors convulsing blowing bed
livid lava founts splash silvery white and red

months and months year after year
cuddling spooning crawling falling
gasping clasping urges forestalling
Clio watching reckoning recording
months and months year after year

smells sweaty hardened decanted too long
hearts racing swollen unzipped dancing prong
biting lips gulping sticky embers ravening tongue

months and months year after year
cuddling spooning crawling falling
gasping clasping urges forestalling
Clio watching reckoning recording
months and months year after year

heaving breathing sipping streaming
a coiled melange melded dreaming
time balloons moons in sky beaming

months and months year after year
cuddling spooning crawling falling
gasping clasping urges forestalling
Clio watching reckoning recording
months and months year after year

mattress drippy rusty bedsprings sprung
bare spots where ripped clothes were flung
once more before reaping daisies in dung

months and months year after year
cuddling spooning crawling falling
gasping clasping urges forestalling
Clio watching reckoning recording
months and months year after year

Hot??? © a year ago, Brad Gilmore

ENTWINED

your aroma pricks with honeysuckle bouquets
ocean on your chestnut face
blinking mahogany dilated orbs
encased in auburn cups fine paintbrush lashes
shimmering skin tight as a drum
smile launching a thousand ships with milky teeth

O how adhesive to each sense and thought you are
beefcake muscles and six-pack abs
who engineered this man with steady character
just man with eyes puddled with rivers
waterfalls cascading and splashing down
from chin to ground
oblivious to the butter churn of social events
we are honey on the honeycomb

Rose petaled pillows dance around our heads
slippery with sweat upon abutting thighs
geysers of molasses-thick fluid
rapidly loads on satin sheets
while biting lips in ecstasy
hugging tight as bears do
entwined in a single energy
discovering a slow boil is better
than a flash in the pan

Wait for the bud to bloom
before thieving it and before the fruit has been birthed[53]

© a year ago, Brad Gilmore

MAKING LOVE IN MINE FIELDS (A TRIBUTE TO LOVERS IN BATTLE'S WASTELAND)

love undercover of shards and rubble
blankets spread over mines and trouble
spears and daggers in the crowded waste
naked bodies chest to chest, face to face

wed 'neath the diamonds of nights' starry lattice
live warm skin moving piqued to semen status
drenched, sobbing eyes with a throbbing pulse
discovered nude scarred, scared by each impulse

soldiers trounce on lovers' aching sweet repose
troops reviling, exploiting an embraced kiss expose
to stone bursting rose blooms while intertwined
on the thorny bush, the pale pair's ardor refined

Whate'er reason for ripping the couple into
and bludgeoning the lovers black and blue,
through each blaze of flame and waves assailed
love is love and each time's prevailed.

How many hidden couples through strife and war have died in each other's arms? No matter the gender, age or race, the triumph of love shames the face of hate. Be champions of mercy, pursue love and love your mate without fear despite the shards of wrath. Hope is kindled each time you do. © 9 months ago, Brad Gilmore

SOLITARY

clock ticks
dragging seconds
in pairs
to fill the hour's bucket

tapping fingertips
indenting the table

bloodshot eyes
24 circular liturgies
stony shadows
mired at twilight

twigs snap
my confinement
no longer solitary

Waiting for my love to come home after years of journey
away © 11 months ago, Brad Gilmore

APRICOT NECTARS

apricot nectars lips induce
vapors from the flame
not touching our eyes

lips wildly parted
paddling tongue tickles
attacks like wolf's maw

dilating saucers
sky lark dry bonds
flushed sunset warm

entwined
petting spooning
panting sweating

© a year ago, Brad Gilmore

ALLOY BLOCKING DISUNION

suckled
parched
no wedding
dread only
flicker depletion
separation

the pocket
rattled
disenchanted

hot breath halting
cheese curdling
puddles of whey
abreadst but far
separation

the coins in pocket
rattled
disenchanted

Alloy
dogwood flower
cranberry rivers
malleable steel
Ocean's Mist
union

Searched high and long, far and wide the security, stability and satisfaction of a life-long companion, soul-mate and lover. But as I and they are transient seekers at best, the One Who sought me from distant heavenly shores is Heart of my heart, Flesh of my flesh.

THE VOICE OF THE
UNUTTERABLE SINGS

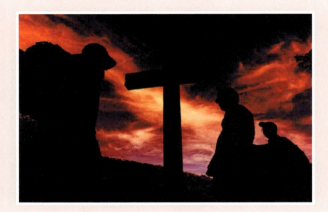

third stone from the sun
upon you the King of Glory comes
shattering bold towers
melting mountains into
drowning wax puddles
on ground-swelling apostasies

Lift up your heads all you gates
and be lifted up you everlasting doors
that the King of Glory may come in

in sky's parchment inky and void
the book of the heavens unfolds
letters as high as galaxies
solar systems are crossed t's
æons of millennia slow and halt
the Voice of the Unutterable sings

Lift up your heads all you gates
and be lifted up you everlasting doors
that the King of Glory may come in

tarred Fate's dark thrusting spear
rattles upon the Ancient door's chamber
demanding to sweep the stars
under his astral, bullet-studded belt
and bastinado angels of the morn
blasting the bursa of Gabriel's humility

Lift up your heads all you gates
and be lifted up you everlasting doors
that the King of Glory may come in

the Archangel blares the terrifying trumpet
God the Judge, God the Merciful One's gavel strikes
one minute past midnight on Eternity's watch
earth and the heavens exchange blows
fragments sheared of what was before
mere chaff blown atomized beyond description

Lift up your heads all you gates
and be lifted up you everlasting doors
that the King of Glory may come in

As archaic heavens expire and
earth's core has turned to ash
The Slain One named the Victory
steps in rending the skies in two
He utters the unutterable
\a new cosmos is born
Satan's rule is vanquished!

Lift up your heads all you gates*
and be lifted up you everlasting doors
that the King of Glory may come in

"'Behold, I make all things new'"**
* see Psalm 24:7, 9; Luke 21:29;
** Revelation 21:1-7

I believe the earth and cosmos as we know it will aflame at the end of this creation. However, my belief goes beyond that the while the old creation is being devoured and skies rolled back as a scroll, a new creation from God will come which only the Lord Jesus can bring ...He will make all things new...there will be a period of utmost calamity and devastation, then a new earth with God-changed people. God will be tabernacled with us. © a year ago, Brad Gilmore

SHRAPNEL OF THE CANOPY

Seventeen years
of wedding rings
and marriage vows
blown to smithereens
wreckage on children spilt.

Through waves
and on deep waters
relation"ship" glided
agony of barely a greenback
dove-fed in the cave

Family expanded
with additions year by year
hours of employment
doubled, tripled
spouse raised the kids
I 'brought home the bacon'

then wealth cascaded in
robbing sewn-together family
distance from pennilessness
bought fetters of dollars
making no sense
the noose tightended
sweet talk turned slurred and biting

my increasing ascendancy
raised the gallows
smothered with clothes and house
strangulation by the "a lot of"
broke the neck of chuppah*
shattered canopy into shrapnel
dismembered cognates**cognates are descendents fro a commoncognates are blood related
dispersion

fragmentation accumulates
starving beatific*** vision
divorced
stamped"incompatible"
a caritas**** nerve remains
but home destroyed

*chuppah= canopy for wedded couple
**cognates= relatives from a common ancestor, thus refers to my children
***beatific= blissful happiness also a Christian blessing; Jewish equivalent might be
"shalom"
****caritas= charity, Christian love for human kind

Divorce from my spouse now for 23 years, but heart remains rent due to love and desirous affections
for her. We are quite good friends now but vision for rekindling and resurrecting the vows between
is passed hope. © a year ago, Brad Gilmore love • sad • divorce • family
Like (2)

THE TILES ON THE FLOOR

Checker were the times we dance upon
Slow and naked skin to skin
Muscles tighten and gently
You lay me upon the tiles black and white
We too lovers one dark and the other fair
Your tongue gives alertness between my thighs
I wrap my parted legs
across your lower chestnut perfect hips
rubbing deeper. we moan softly
encircling you with arched curling my toes

My mouth says pantingly
You, whose eyes are blue as the sky,
Seeing souls and bodies amalgamated
Hard as steel and rocking rhythmically
As the heaving becomes
more perfect than the one before
each one from whimpers to sweet cry
As we spill over like glaze on duck
Our flesh goose flesh
our bodies blushed

Entwined upon the tiles on floor
Red skin upon the black and white tiles.

This a way to express the eros inside to my mate. I hope it was gentle sparking desire for the one you love and cherish. © 2 years ago, Brad Gilmore